THE SECRET POEMS

Jessie Vong

First published by Busybird Publishing 2025

Copyright © 2025 Jessie Vong

ISBN:
Paperback: 978-1-923216-79-2
Ebook: 978-1-923216-80-8

This book is copyright. Apart from any fair dealing for the purposes of study, research, criticism, review, or as otherwise permitted under the Copyright Act, no part may be reproduced by any process without written permission. Enquiries should be made through the publisher.

This is a work of fiction. Any similarities between places and characters are a coincidence.

Cover image: Jessie Vong

Cover design: Jessie Vong

Layout and typesetting: Busybird Publishing

Illustrations: Jessie Vong

Busybird Publishing
2/118 Para Road
Montmorency, Victoria
Australia 3094
www.busybird.com.au

BIOGRAPHY

About the Author: Jessie Vong

Jessie Vong is an emerging artist and poet, currently pursuing Art Therapy studies at the College of Complementary Medicine in NSW, Australia, a journey she began in October 2024. With a passion for creativity and mental health advocacy, Jessie's work bridges the worlds of art and healing, inspired by her deep belief that art is "food for the soul."

Her poetry journey began when her art therapy lecturers recognized her talent and encouraged her to publish a book combining insightful verses with her personable hand-drawn illustrations. This creative endeavor reflects her dedication to expressing abstract thoughts and emotions, encouraging readers to reflect, grow, and discover new perspectives.

Jessie holds a Certificate IV in Mental Health and Post Graduate Studies in Counselling and plans to further her studies in Art Therapy. Her compassionate and empathetic nature is evident in her work, which often explores themes of calmness, contemporary ideas, and postmodern romanticism. By combining poetic expression with artistic detail, Jessie's creations resonate with a global audience, unravelling complex emotions in a world of constant radical change.

Through her art and writing, Jessie aims to inspire self-reflection and mindfulness, helping others navigate and meditate on their own personal journeys while fostering a positive impact on society from acquiring wisdom and or achieving a new perspective to influence the individual's sense of meaning and "self."

Poems

Heart Work	1
Wonderment	2
Even Then	3
They Don't Just	4
Plan for It	6
So Good	7
Beautiful Detail	8
Product Of	9
Highest Expression	10
Cosmic Heart	11
Higher Power	12
Take the Line	13
Celestial Queen	14
Walking Manifester	15
My Gift	16
Blessed Me	17
Wow	18
I Agreed	19
I Am the Most Powerful	20
To Seem	21
To Be Her	22
The Preparation	23
Just Be Patient	24
Cinderella Moment	25
Mindset	26
I Want to Leave	27
You Should Consider	28

Stronger Than Anything	29
State of Flow	30
Dreams Soar	31
Give It Back	32
Another Reason	33
They Never Knew	34
Fighter Lover	35
Give You Rest	36
Swag	37
Trophy Wife	38
Save Yourself	39
Cutest Thing	40
I Don't Even Care	41
Reborn	42
Curse Reverse	43
Marked	44
Minding My Business	46
Playing Games	48
When Toxic	50
Defending Kingdom	51
Thoughts of Affection	53
To Be the Creative	55
Paid to Exist	57
Lovesick Puppy	58
Keep It	60
More Prosperous	62
Even More	63
Star of the Show	64

Heart Work

The heart beats—steady, resilient, alive,
A rhythm that whispers the essence of life.
It awakens in silence, stirred by the unknown,
A chamber of wisdom, where seeds of truth are sown.

The heart listens—softly, beyond spoken word,
Catching the unvoiced, the cries that go unheard.
It learns with each moment, from joy and despair,
Expanding with love, or cradling what's unfair.

The heart opens—a flower in bloom,
Dispelling the darkness, enlightening the gloom.
It enlightens with courage, it glows with its might,
Guiding the soul through shadows to light.

For the beating of the heart is more than a sound,
It's a call to connection, a truth profound.
And the necessity is this: to let the heart work,
To feel, to awaken, to rise from the murk.

So let it beat, let it open, let it learn and impart,
For life's greatest labor is the work of the heart.

Wonderment

I wonder why you misunderstood me,
A quiet truth lost in the chaos of words.
I wonder why I gaze into your eyes,
Seeking the depths where your essence stirs.

I gaze into your soul—boundless, infinite,
Your soul and my soul, intertwined in virtue.
Yet, I wonder why you turned away,
Why silence became the thread we pursue.

I wonder why you ignored me,
When my presence was a lighthouse in your storm.
I wonder why I forgave your soul,
Offering solace to the wounds that conform.

Your character and my charm, a virtue shared,
A balance of energies meant to heal.
Yet, I wonder why mistrust emerged,
A shadow that dulled what once felt real.

I wonder why I tried with you,
Holding on when the tide pulled us apart.
Your trust and my loyalty, a virtue rare,
A fragile bridge between two hearts.

And so, I wonder in wonderment,
A reflection that echoes without end.
For in the labyrinth of why, I find myself,
Seeking the meaning, time cannot bend.

Even Then

Even then, even when
My feet touch the solid ground,
Even then, even when
My body greets the open air.

Even then, even when
Each outbreath I take
Becomes a moment of relief,
A chance to replenish what is bare.

Even then, even when
I sit, and my body grows heavier,
Drawn deeper into the earth's embrace.
Even then, even when
I feel the charm resting within me,
A quiet light, a sacred grace.

Even then, even when
I recall my grandmother's voice,
Her wisdom radiating, steady and true.
Even then, even when
The world seems to hush—
Peaceful, drifting, heartfelt anew.

Even then, even when
The surroundings whisper their presence,
The breeze brushing softly across my skin.
Even then, even when
I step into my sacred space,
A stillness blooms from within.

Even then, even when
I see that all I need is here,
In this moment, perfectly aligned.
Even then, even when
Yours, ours, and my timing
Are harmonized, synchronized, refined.

They Don't Just

They don't just make sense—
They unravel the threads of logic,
Twisting understanding into something
Wild and untamed, beyond reason's grasp.

They don't just see the truth—
They pierce it, break it open,
Expose the fragile heart within,
Daring it to beat amidst chaos.

They don't just become spellbound—
They conjure magic in the mundane,
Dancing on the edge of enchantment,
Where wonder feels like breathing fire.

They are reckless—
A storm unyielding,
Tearing through the walls of stillness,
Demanding to be felt, to be known.

The need for recklessness is relentless—
A hunger clawing at the edges of order,
A thirst unquenchable, a flame unextinguished.

The need for calming after the storms
Propels one into sanity,
But only just enough to rebuild
The ruins left behind.

Their need is for my presence—
Not as a mere witness,
But as the anchor in their tempest,
The quiet in their chaos.

But they don't just—
They don't simply exist.
They burn, they crash,
They transform everything they touch
Into something infinite.

Plan for It

Plan for the journey,
A step into the unknown,
Leave the answers of the past behind,
For seeds already sown.

Project into the future,
Where fleeting desires fade,
The things of lust may not endure,
But hope will never jade.

Project to feel,
To root yourself in the present.
An undecided path still leads somewhere,
Its meaning ever crescent.

Project into the now,
Where the heavens open wide,
An infinite expanse of possibility,
A place where truth resides.

So Good

So good, you brought comfort to my storms,
Where discomfort once raged, your presence transforms.
So good, you helped me find my hidden light,
Guiding me gently, turning darkness to bright.

So good, you held the pieces of my soul,
Through your care and love, I became whole.
So good, you heard the cries I tried to hide,
Listening deeply, standing by my side.

So good, you ignored the whispers of lies,
Holding on to truth, where strength and hope arise.
So good, so endlessly good of you,
To heal, to love, and to see me through.

Beautiful Detail

Beautiful woman, graceful and bright,
Beautiful man, a soul full of light.
Beautiful child, with eyes full of wonder,
Beautiful infant, innocence like thunder.

Beautifulness lies deep within,
In hearts where true beauty begins.
Tranquil and calm, it finds its start,
In the quiet corners of the heart.

Beauty aligns with the highs we climb,
Adorning mirrors with visions sublime.
A chameleon stare, both bold and rare,
Ambitious, creative, beyond compare.

Your beauty, mine, and all that we share,
A rare and fleeting treasure, precious and fair.
Beauty in these details, so true, so deep,
In every glance, in all that we keep.

Product Of

You are a product of society,
A reflection of all that we see.
A product of your upbringing,
Where lessons and pain are deeply clinging.

Full of hypnotic strains and sway,
It taps deep into your veins each day.
As we bleed through trials and trauma's pain,
We find peace that cannot be contained.

Beyond all borders, beyond all fears,
A product of struggles, shedding tears.
A matrix system, tightly bound,
But freedom waits when we listen and sound.

From being heard, to standing tall,
The product of self-worth, breaking walls.
Here we are, unearthed and whole,
A product of growth, a liberated soul.

Therefore, we are the product of...
Society's hold, but also of love.

Plan for the past,
The lessons it has taught.
Plan for the present,
Where battles must be fought.

Plan for the future,
Where dreams await their chance.
Just plan for it—
The journey's worth the dance.. Just plan

Highest Expression

I am my highest expression,
A soul in endless progression.
I am my highest untapped force,
Guided by an inner course.

I am my highest genius bright,
Shining through the darkest night.
I am my greatest forgiveness,
Healing wounds with tender sweetness.

I am my greatest discovery,
Unlocking truths in life's mystery.
I am my greatest lovingly,
Embracing all that comes to me.

I am my profound nature, deep,
Rooted where the mysteries sleep.
I am my profound dictator,
Guiding myself with love, not later.

I am my profound guide,
In the heavens, where dreams collide.
I am my highest, greatest, and profound,
In every step, I am unbound.

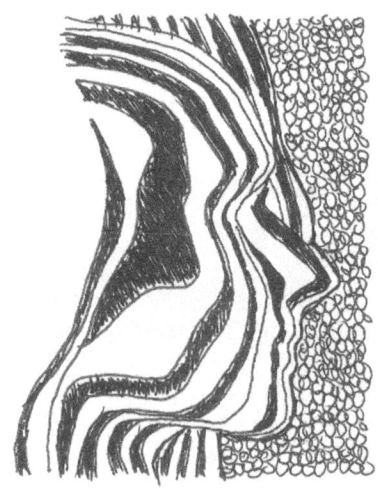

Cosmic Heart

I have a cosmic heart,
A boundless force, a work of art.
My cosmic heart is full with pleasure,
A treasure beyond all earthly measure.

My consciousness of heart unties what's bound,
Making sense of all the souls I've found.
My cosmic heart is healed, restored, concealed,
In its vastness, all wounds are sealed.

My cosmic heart feels into the universe,
Bringing light where dark thoughts disperse.
Levels of love, they traverse and soar,
Endless beauty forevermore.

My cosmic heart radiates magic bright,
A consistent glow, forever alight.
Something constant, that's never tragic,
I have a cosmic heart, so pure, so magic.

Higher Power

Lift me up, for I am higher power,
Rising strong in this sacred hour.
Lift me up, for I am forsaken,
Yet in this moment, I am awakened.

Release the energies, wild and free,
Release what is meant to be.
Fill me with what's required to grow,
From now until the end, let it flow.

Higher power, graceful and true,
Makes my life magical, anew.
A light full of glory, shining bright,
Destined to be free from all fright.

No sin, no prejudice, no dismay,
For in higher power, I find my way.
No worries, no fears to devour,
For I am guided by higher power.

Take the Line

You take the cue to take the line,
Unwavering steps, where paths entwine.
Take the line to nurture nature,
For all things align in favor's gesture.

Take the line to be sublime,
Mix with the crowd, and surface in time.
Take the line, embrace what's new,
For in its flow, great things will brew.

And as it rattles, others too,
Take the line, feel daring and true.
Feel bare, with love and care,
For Mother Nature's lair is everywhere.

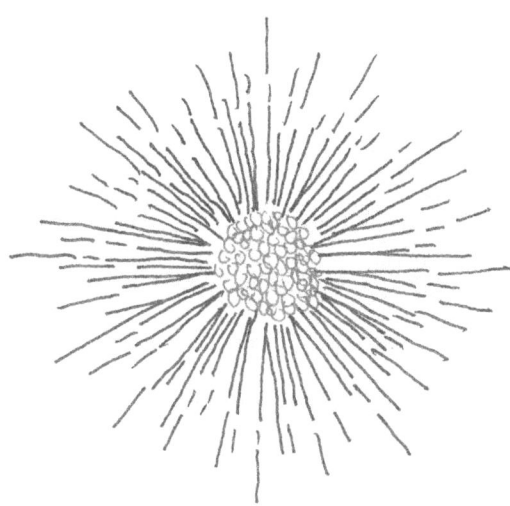

Celestial Queen

I am Goddess, I am Divine,
A Celestial Queen, beyond time.
To live a life I could ever dream,
A radiant force, a sacred beam.

To cast out the bad, to rise above,
Reviving with the sad, through endless love.
Breaking even with what's said to be mad,
Finding peace in all that I've had.

I am keen to be queen,
To be seen in the light serene.
If only you knew, if only you'd see,
The power it takes to be Celestial Queen, like me.

Walking Manifester

I walk to be seen,
I walk to be serene.
I come in peace,
To heal and to release.

With care, I handle myself and stare,
Gazing into the future, unaware.
In my own existence, I find my place,
Making hope bloom in every space.

Hope for plenty, hope for grace,
A life of serenity in its embrace.
I walk a path of valid talk,
Becoming all that universal laws unlock.

I am the walking manifester,
A dreamer, a doer, a truth confessing tester.

My Gift

I have a gift,
A secret only I know,
A treasure that glows,
Of whispers and heavenly bows.

This gift, I nurture with care,
In every moment, I learn to prepare.
I learn to grow, to feel, to rise,
To kneel in reverence, with open eyes.

To the most high, I bow in grace,
Letting jealousy fade from my embrace.
In precarious waters, I drift and float,
Carrying the ember of hope in my throat.

Not knowing what to hide, I stand,
With trust in the power to guide my hand.
I believe, with every step I take,
That I hold the choice to make or break.

I have the power of discernment,
To see beyond what's evident.
I have the power of justice, pure and true,
To right the wrongs, and start anew.

I have the power of truth, my light,
Shining through the darkest night.
I have the power of validation,
To affirm my soul, my worth, my station.

For within me lies this sacred gift,
A force so strong, it can shift.
I have the gift, I hold it tight, A beacon of strength, a guiding light

Blessed Me

I am the blessed one,
A soul under the rising sun.
Grateful for the purpose you gave,
Grateful for the strength you helped me crave.

I am grateful for you believing in me,
Even when the world refused to see.
Grateful for the hurt you put me through,
For now, I stand my ground, and hold what is true.

I am a one-woman show,
A force that no one can overthrow.
This world, it's mine, not yours to blow,
I've learned to rise, to let it all flow.

Feelings of disbelief, once strong,
Now fade, like a forgotten song.
How love, prosperity, and gifts bring relief,
I am healed, I am free from grief.

The things that were said are now dead,
Faded whispers of what once spread.
Now, so suddenly, I seek something new,
The life I have is rare and for a few.

Unbelievingly, yet believingly,
I hold my faith in what I've yet to see.
For I am the blessed one, so full of grace,
I embrace my life, my heart, my place.

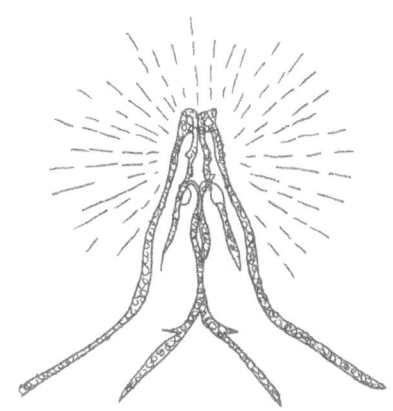

Wow

I love the way you just say "wow,"
It echoes through my heart, here and now.
Wow is in your nature, pure and true,
A spark in your soul that lights up the view.

Wow is in your reach, within your grasp,
A power that flows, a light in your clasp.
Wow is how you speak, each word so profound,
A rhythm so sweet, a beautiful sound.

Wow is a wonderment, beyond compare,
A magic that dances in the open air.
Wow, that you manifest, cultivates elements,
Bringing life to dreams with no impediments.

The wow elements you gracefully show,
Are proof of the beauty in letting things flow.
You move with ease, a heart full of grace,
A living testament to life's embrace.

In love with the way you wow,
I stand in awe, I humbly vow.
Speechless, I am, as your energy lifts,
A force that soars, a celestial gift.

I love the way you wow, it leaves me amazed,
A wonder in your presence, I'm truly dazed.
Every word, every action, a tale untold,
In the way you wow, so bold, so gold.

I Agreed

I told you I had agreed,
Agreed to this plan, so carefully laid,
I had agreed to this pain,
To walk through the storms, the endless rain.

I had agreed to this suffering,
To bear the weight, to keep uncovering,
But within it all, I found my grace,
A golden age, my destined place.

For I had agreed it will be my time,
To rise above, to feel sublime.
With strength renewed, my heart shall shine,
I shall rise and confide in those I love, divine.

With memories I treasure, stored in the sky,
Whispers from above, they never die.
The downloads are real, they touch my soul,
A deep connection, making me whole.

I had agreed to this fate,
To walk this path, to open the gate.
I had agreed to vacate,
Leaving behind the old, embracing what's great.

To a place of paradise, so serene,
Where the air is pure, where all is seen.
To a place of enigma, mysterious and bright,
Where everything aligns in perfect light.

I stand tall to forgive her,
Release the past, no longer deter.
With peace in my heart and love in my eyes,
I let go of the pain, to soar to the skies.

For I had agreed, and now I stand,
A soul reborn, with a steady hand.
The journey continues, the future is mine,A golden age, by design.

I Am the Most Powerful

It's hard to believe, but I am the most powerful,
A force unshaken, pure and bountiful.
A heart that holds, that never sways,
A power deep, lighting the way.

It's hard to believe, but I have a place,
In the corners of my heart, to keep our grace.
A space where distance will not tear,
Where love and strength are always there.

It's hard to believe, yet here I stand,
Firm in my truth, with heart in hand.
I grieve, yes, but through the pain,
I rise again, embracing the gain.

For my power gives me luck untold,
Abundance and truth in sleeves of gold.
New opportunities to embrace,
A life where I hold the power and grace.

I am the most powerful, for views I renew,
I see the world in a light that's true.
I am the most powerful, with courage anew,
Beginning again, with strength to pursue.

In the search for relentlessness, deep within,
I find the strength to begin again.
I rise, I fall, but always stand tall,
For in my soul, there's nothing too small.

I am the most powerful in newfound glory,
A tale of redemption, rewriting my story.
Avoiding the shadows, embracing the light,
I walk with grace, free from the night.

Makes my happiness take shape, so free,
I am the author of my destiny.
I am so powerful, it's my truth to claim,
A force of nature, forever to remain.

To Seem

I like to seem like something sometimes,
A reflection of grace in my quiet rhymes.
I like to seem humble, a soul at rest,
A calm in the chaos, a heart truly blessed.

I like to seem gentle, like the softest breeze,
Whispering peace, with effortless ease.
I like to seem classy, refined and pure,
A presence that lingers, calm and sure.

I like to seem authentic, true to my core,
A spirit unbroken, yearning for more.
I like to seem relentlessly searching for truth,
The answers that guide me, from days of youth.

The answers I seek lie deep in my prayer,
In moments of stillness, when none are there.
I am not alone, but sometimes I feel,
The weight of the world, too heavy to heal.

I like to seem like I know what to do,
But sometimes, I find I must start anew.
To give myself a break and wine down mad stares,
To retreat in solitude and breathe in the air.

For the company I have, I cherish so dear,
Those whose love is a melody I hold near.
I like to seem to have a few as a sign,
Those who reflect the divine, who truly shine.

The company I keep is a genuine crew,
Blessed to walk with those who see life through.
Makes life seem anew, full of grace and glow,
As we journey together, letting love freely flow.

To Be Her

To be me as her is challenging,
A puzzle of strength, endlessly managing.
To be her is beautiful, a vision divine,
A soul that shines like a radiant sign.

To be her is graceful, like a quiet breeze,
Floating through moments with effortless ease.
To be her is sanity, a calm in the storm,
A steady heart that keeps me warm.

To be her is magical, like a dream untold,
A wonder of courage, fierce and bold.
To be her is full of light, a flame that glows,
A beacon of hope wherever she goes.

To be her is a work of art,
A masterpiece crafted from the heart.
The art is refined, with every brushstroke neat,
A symphony of beauty, bittersweet.

The art is creative, a burst of new ideas,
A journey of innovation that conquers fears.
The art is manipulative, weaving through time,
Shaping the world with rhythm and rhyme.

The art is peaceful and complacent, yet addictive,
A force that comforts, while being restrictive.
I am myself as her, complex and true,
A blend of strength, softness, and hues.

To be her is to embrace it all,
The highs, the lows, the rise and fall.
For in being her, I find my own worth,
A reflection of who I am from birth.

The Preparation

I must prepare,
For what is coming, a future so fair.
A journey ahead, unknown yet clear,
The path will unfold, but I must persevere.

I must prepare for the awakening,
A shift of mind, a heart reshaping.
The awakening of truths, deep and vast,
As I step into light, letting go of the past.

I must prepare to teach, learn, and grow,
To nurture the seeds, and let wisdom flow.
Manifesting dreams, with every step I take,
Transforming the world for humanity's sake.

I must prepare to love unconditionally,
To open my heart, without hesitation or frantically.
Love that transcends all barriers and fears,
Love that heals, that nurtures, that clears.

I must prepare to take the agreed assignment,
A mission entrusted, a divine alignment.
The task ahead is mine to unfold,
A story of courage, of truth to be told.

I must acknowledge the truth in love, light, and darkness,
Embracing each part, without hesitation or starkness.
For in darkness, we find the lessons to see,
And in the light, we discover who we're meant to be.

For I have the preparation to learn and guide discernment,
To look through the veil, with wisdom so permanent.
The wisdom to know when to lead and when to follow,
The strength to embrace both joy and sorrow.

This is my preparation, a calling so pure,
A journey of faith, of love that's sure.
With every breath, I'm ready to embrace,
The unfolding of time, with grace and with pace.

Just Be Patient

Just be patient, and hold on tight,
For life is worth living, through day and night.
In moments of doubt, when shadows loom near,
Just be patient, for the light will appear.

Hold onto new-found glory, so bright,
As the world beneath me shifts with stories alight.
Every turn, a new chapter unfolds,
Patience reveals the secrets it holds.

Just be patient, as you look all adoring,
In awe of this world, so vast and exploring.
This place, this space, whispers to your soul,
"Just be patient," as it helps you unfold.

Patience takes time, it's an art so divine,
We make the time, like stars that align.
Don't rush the process, let it be,
For in patience, you find your key.

There is a safe haven, waiting for you,
A place of peace, where dreams come true.
This gift, laden with wisdom and grace,
Is found in patience, in life's sacred space.

Though all things quarrel, and tempers may rise,
Just be patient, and you'll soon realize,
The beauty in waiting, the power to see,
That patience is the doorway to being free.

So just be patient, and trust the way,
For in time, all will find its place to stay.
A gentle reminder, through life's ebb and flow,
Just be patient, and let your spirit grow.

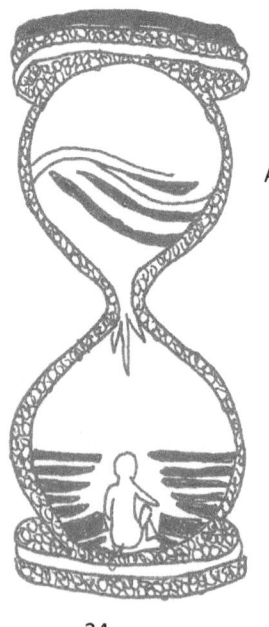

Cinderella Moment

I have a Cinderella moment, shining bright,
A woman awakened, stepping into the light.
I've become someone worthy of the show,
A story of strength, for all to know.

I've listened to what my mama knows,
Her wisdom, like seeds, in my heart it grows.
My nanna taught me grace, with every stride,
A gentle strength, I wear with pride.

My dad showed me faith, unwavering and true,
A beacon of light that guided me through.
I carry his love, a light in my soul,
A piece of his strength, making me whole.

I know it is heavenly, this glow I feel,
A radiant warmth, undeniably real.
I summon the owls, and the birds take flight,
Their wings bring wisdom, guiding me right.

My dreams, like stars, now fill the sky,
Abundant with luck, soaring high.
I know that my future is here to unfold,
In this Cinderella moment, I feel bold.

Here on earth, and in the heavenly realms,
My journey continues, as destiny overwhelms.
I walk in grace, with faith as my guide,
A woman of power, no longer to hide.

In this Cinderella moment, I rise and stand,
A reflection of love, with strength in my hands.
For I am the magic, the dream come true,
A woman transformed, shining through.

Mindset

It is in my powerful mindset,
A force unseen, but never regret.
I am because of what I believe,
For my mindset is what I achieve.

My mindset is strong, unshaken by time,
A steady rhythm, a perfect rhyme.
It holds within it, a pure intention,
Guiding my heart with steady direction.

My mindset carries burdens, deep and true,
Lessons learned and paths to pursue.
It holds the weight of battles fought,
Of dreams built and lessons taught.

My mindset carries secrets, quiet and deep,
Whispering truths that I vow to keep.
It holds the key to parts untold,
A sacred space where thoughts unfold.

My mindset carries mystery, untamed,
A wild spirit that can't be framed.
It dances with shadows, speaks with the stars,
Unraveling the universe, both near and far.

Although my mindset is composed of these things,
It is also free, like the wind that sings.
No chains to bind, no walls to break,
It soars above, for its own sake.

My mindset is free, like a bird in flight,
A canvas of thoughts, a boundless light.
It chooses its path, with courage and grace,
A limitless force in this sacred space.

For in my powerful mindset, I find my way,
It is the compass that guides me each day.
A strength that endures, a fire that stays,
My mindset is mine, in all of its ways.

I Want to Leave

I've decided it's time—I want to leave,
To slip through the cracks of what you believe.
I want to leave you hanging, lost in thought,
A puzzle unsolved, a lesson I taught.

I want to leave you guessing, chasing my trace,
A fleeting shadow, an unclaimed space.
I want to leave you behind with the past,
To shed the weight that couldn't last.

I am an enigma, a mystery untold,
A spark of fire, both fierce and bold.
I need to leave, to wander, to roam,
To find the place where my spirit calls home.

No one can define me, for I am vast,
A chameleon's colors that shift so fast.
No one can cage me or clip my wings,
For I am the rhythm the wild wind sings.

No one can object to the path I tread,
For I've written my story in ink that's bled.
No one can hold me, no one can see,
The limitless force that's rooted in me.

So, I'll leave with grace, no need to grieve,
I am not lost—I've chosen to leave.
To journey forward, untethered and free,
In the endless expanse where I'm meant to be.

You Should Consider

You should consider these things, my friend,
The truths that linger, the hearts that bend.
You should consider one's fleeting presence,
The moments they offer, their quiet essence.

You should consider one's greater purpose,
The depth of their soul, beneath the surface.
Each life is a book with pages to read,
You should consider their stories indeed.

You should consider the bonds that tether,
The fragile threads that hold us together.
One's need for another, the comfort they seek,
A hand to hold when the world feels bleak.

Instead of judging with eyes so blind,
You should consider a heart more kind.
Empathy blooms where understanding grows,
A simple act that every soul knows.

You should consider, for life's a shared art,
Each person a piece, a work from the heart.
To love, to connect, to lift and to see,
You should consider, and simply *be*.

Stronger Than Anything

I feel it deep within my soul,
A power that keeps me whole.
Stronger than anything you place in my way,
A force that grows brighter with each passing day.

Anything you set to block my path,
I'll rise above, defying your wrath.
Anything you try to disrupt in my art,
Will only deepen the fire in my heart.

Anything you fumble to strike with harsh might,
Becomes a lesson that sharpens my light.
Anything to mock or tear me apart,
Becomes the fuel that ignites my start.

Every hurdle, every storm,
Shaping my strength, transforming my form.
For in every ending, I find a beginning,
In every battle, my soul keeps winning.

I am stronger than anything you bring,
A force unyielding, a soul that sings.
No weight too heavy, no night too long,
I am unbreakable—I am strong.

State of Flow

The state of flow is where I reside,
A peaceful place where dreams abide.
A gentle rhythm, a soothing stream,
Where life aligns like a vivid dream.

The state of flow makes all things clear,
A magical space where doubts disappear.
It's where intentions manifest with grace,
A boundless, infinite, creative place.

In this state, imagination soars,
Opening wide celestial doors.
A dance of thoughts, a spark of light,
Guiding the soul through day and night.

The state of flow is where we meet,
As counterparts, our energies greet.
A mirror of growth, a reflective art,
A sacred rhythm that binds each heart.

Here, time dissolves, and truth will show,
All things align in the state of flow.
It carries me, it lets me be,
A vessel of endless possibility.

Dreams Soar

Dreams appear like whispers in the night,
Bathed in mystery, kissed by light.
Dreams of fantasy, where wonders grow,
A tapestry of worlds we'll never outgrow.

Dreams of realms, vast and untold,
Through cosmic skies, through stars of gold.
Dreams soar high through the multi-verses,
Writing their tales in infinite verses.

Dreams materialize from the spirit's desire,
Shaping worlds with ethereal fire.
From heavens above, they begin to descend,
Where magic and reality beautifully blend.

Dreams of you and I, bound by fate,
Our love eternal, no time can abate.
In the dreamscape, our souls always meet,
Dancing to rhythms steady and sweet.

The dreaming soars, an endless flight,
Guided by hope, embraced by light.
Through realms of wonder, bold and free,
Dreams soar and weave our destiny.

Give It Back

Give it back, the threads I helped you weave,
A tapestry of kindness, you chose to deceive.
Give it back to the sender, let justice flow,
Return the grace, let your heart grow.

Give it back, in gestures true,
Seek deliverance, a life renewed.
The helping hands I once adorned,
Now ache with loss, forlorn and scorned.

The savage way you stole from me,
Left echoes of pain, a silent plea.
Give it back, not just the things you take,
But honor, trust, for my soul's sake.

I mourn the love you left to lack,
And still, I pray—just give it back.
Give it back, with solemn grace,
Restore the light in this empty space.

Another Reason

I will give you another reason,
To mend the cracks of this fleeting season.
I will give you another chance,
To join me in our solidarity dance.

But don't ever call it even,
For trust takes time, like the changing seasons.
Another reason to see you through,
Another reason to forgive, renew.

Another reason for transparency's light,
Another reason to battle the night.
I sacrifice plans, let go of my stance,
Another reason to give love a chance.

Another reason to reason myself,
To pull hope from the shadowed shelf.
If only you'd knowingly understand,
This reason is fragile, placed in your hand.

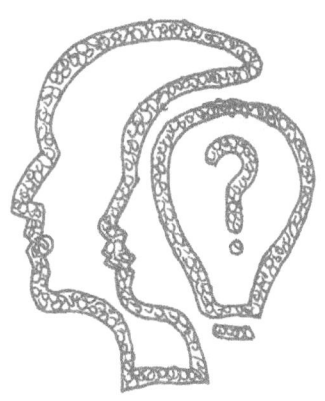

They Never Knew

I think they never knew the truth,
The hidden spark that lies in youth.
I think they never thought to see,
The power held inside of me.

I think they never believed I'd rise,
That I'd outshine their hollow lies.
I think they never did need faith,
To walk the path that heaven makes.

Yet belief is strong, and sight is keen,
Through shadows dark and spaces between.
Such a gift to see your night,
Yet greater still, to see your light.

My life is lit, a burning flame,
Through your remorse and quiet shame.
I think they grew from spiteful calls,
And either built or broke their walls.

For every door that closed me out,
Another opened, without doubt.
The kingdom's truth revealed their flaws,
Their hollow crowns, their brittle laws.

Hang on tight, the path is steep,
But treasures lie in what you keep.
The journey's bright, a boundless flight,
Although they never knew my light.

Fighter Lover

I will fight for your love, steadfast and true,
Through storms of doubt, I'll battle for you.
I will fight for your touch, your affection's flame,
I will fight for your smile, to cherish your name.

I will fight for your gaze, your attention's embrace,
Through heartache's shadow, I'll find my place.
I'll transmute the pain into a fire of passion,
A love that endures, defying aggression.

But please, my love, leave no room for disdain,
No secrets or shadows to deepen the pain.
For there may come a time, temptation may call,
But loyalty's light can conquer it all.

How holy and pure a love can be,
When built on trust, steadfast and free.
You and I, through battles and tears,
Fighter lovers, bound by the years.

Only to me, this truth will remain,
Our love's fierce fire will never wane.
For in the war of hearts, I'll always strive,
To keep our bond eternal, alive.

Give You Rest

I will give you rest when trials abound,
When the weight of the world pulls you to the ground.
I will give you solace when your spirit's distressed,
For every hard question, I'll give you my best.

I will give you power to rise and to fight,
To transform what's bitter into what's right.
I will give you courage to face what you fear,
A guiding light when the path's unclear.

I will give you prayer, a shield in the storm,
A whisper of hope to keep your heart warm.
For every wavering step, I'll steady your pace,
With faith as the anchor, with love as the space.

I will give you time to mend what is torn,
To turn the spilled wine into joy reborn.
I'll offer my testimony, a truth profound,
A source everlasting, in it we're bound.

This is not only your test, it is mine too,
A journey together, we'll both see it through.
For though trials may shake us, we'll pass every quest,
And when it is over, I will give you rest.

Swag

I carry myself with a kind of swagger,
Sharper than steel, like a brand-new dagger.
Though I lag behind in a creative race,
I carve my own path with effortless grace.

Some may see me as a wandering wagger,
But my soul burns brighter, a defiant stagger.
My demeanor is fueled by a love for school,
A cosmic mission, the universe's tool.

With every step, I radiate style,
Gracing the world, mile by mile.
This swag I hold, it's more than a show,
It's a beacon of light wherever I go.

No reason to wag, no need to stray,
My swag guides me through every day.
And though I may boast, it's more than a brag,
It's a call to inspire—to follow my swag.

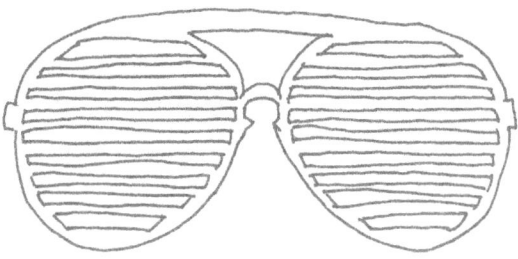

Trophy Wife

I feel like the trophy wife,
A symbol of grace, love, and life.
A partner chosen, heaven's gift,
A bond so pure, the world can't drift.

From birth, my duty began to grow,
A righteous path I've come to know.
With the strength of a mother, a queen divine,
I cradle your heart, as you cradle mine.

I seek the depths where secrets hide,
To share the truth, to walk beside.
You are the man, steadfast and strong,
I am the woman, where dreams belong.

Together we weave a timeless thread,
Evenly woven, well-spun, well-spread.
The magic lingers in every scene,
A love that glows, a beauty pristine.

For I am not just a prize to claim,
I am a partner, steadfast, untamed.
A light that shines in the darkest of night,
For I am your trophy wife, your guiding light.

Save Yourself

You can always try to save yourself,
To reclaim your strength, to build your wealth.
You can always strive to make amends,
To mend the bridges, to heal, to tend.

You can always try to defend,
Your soul, your truth, from start to end.
You can always reach to ascend,
Beyond the storms, where stars extend.

I try my best not to deeply offend,
The fragile balance we must defend.
For peace and light, though fragile in might,
Hold power to soften the darkest night.

The strength you've summoned to save your heights,
To climb the peaks, to face your fights.
A prelude of giving, receiving in kind,
An eternal cycle of heart and mind.

Mutual respect, a sacred sight,
Guides the way through endless night.
The might is strong upon this earth,
A testament to your inner worth.

To save yourself is to truly see,
The boundless potential of what you can be.
And in the quiet, when shadows take flight,
Know saving yourself brings all into light.

Cutest Thing

I think you've seen the cutest thing,
A spark that makes your heart take wing.
I think you'd be keen to know,
To feel the warmth that softly glows.

I beg you, don't be cruel or mean,
Don't let the world dull what's serene.
Don't digress to a place of doubt,
Where self-esteem begins to shout.

I've seen the cutest thing, you see,
A gentle soul that sings to me.
It's pure and bright, a heart that beams,
A living wonder, born of dreams.

This cute thing is lovable, I foresee,
With every glance, it sets hearts free.
It's huggable, a comforting grace,
A tender touch in a hurried race.

In all the chaos, this thing is sweet,
A calming presence, soft and neat.
Nonetheless, this thing remains the seed,
A love that grows, fulfilling need.

The cutest thing, so rare, so true,
A simple joy that shines right through.
It's not in looks, or fleeting trends,
But in the love it always sends.

I Don't Even Care

Tell me about it,
I don't even care.
Make a story, weave your tale,
But I wouldn't even dare.

The thoughts, they run and then they dry,
Like fleeting winds that whisper by.
I watch them fade, I feel the flow,
As magic turns what's old to new.

Through transmutation, my spirit's light,
I love to learn, to find my height.
Creating a haven, a peaceful space,
A sanctuary where I embrace my grace.

They try to gossip, from heir to heir,
But honestly, I don't even care.
Whispers float, but they can't stay,
For I am rising above the fray.

Shout to me your envies, your petty cries,
Tell me all that you can empty from your mind.
For I am not weighed down by despair,
I will show you how I don't even care.

I walk with strength, unbent, unfazed,
In my own world, where peace is raised.
No need for drama, no need for stress,
I choose to live my life with less.

So bring your noise, your twisted stare,
But I'll keep moving, unaware.
For in my heart, I've found a way,
To rise above, to find my sway.

Tell me, tell me, say it loud,
I will not be pulled beneath the cloud.
I'll shine through the storm, unbroken, free,
For I don't even care what they think of me.

Reborn

Make me reborn anew,
With strength and grace in every hue.
Make me rise from the depths below,
A soul transformed, ready to glow.

Make me reborn with a mighty crew,
Together, we'll see a world renewed.
With hearts united, strong and free,
In this new life, we find our key.

Make them reborn for heaven's sake,
With no more sorrow, no more ache.
Let the past fade, leave no mistake,
In the light of this dawn, all hearts awake.

Make them seek rebirth without trouble,
As we emerge from the darkened rubble.
Portraying strength, a second chance,
In the dance of life, we take our stance.

As we peak into the light of day,
Another rebirth is our chosen way.
Each strike, a lesson, each fall, a guide,
In the journey of life, we cannot hide.

Make them reborn, renewed and true,
Let the birthright shine in all we do.
No gloom shall touch this sacred path,
For in this moment, we have found our craft.

Seeking revenge? That's not our tune,
For we rise as one, beneath the moon.
Hold on tight for heaven's sake,
We are reborn to enter the gates.

With open arms, we step inside,
No more fear, no more lies.
In this rebirth, we find our grace,
We are the chosen, in heaven's embrace.

Curse Reverse

I ponder why you curse me,
With words so harsh, so wild, so free.
I wonder why your voice rings loud,
As if to pierce the world's dark cloud.

If you haven't seen my mightiness,
I fear you may be in some distress.
For a force unseen lies deep within,
A power that you cannot begin.

To curse and verse these bitter wishes,
I take thee down to darkened swishes.
Into the depths, where shadows dance,
I claim my strength, I hold my stance.

For coming here with curses bold,
I cast you deep in realms untold.
Your words, like chains, cannot bind,
The light I carry, the peace I find.

The curse, once cast, now falters away,
There is no room for it to stay.
No space to breathe, no air to find,
For justice, truth, is intertwined.

There you lay, in sorrow strained,
Your bitter words, they are in vain.
I hope that justice, calm and true,
Will rise, will shine, and shine anew.

For I have an unwavering ear,
I hear the truth, I know no fear.
Your curse, now gone, has lost its sway,
Reversed in light, it fades away.

The power of peace, the strength of love,
I call upon the stars above.
Your curse is lost, it cannot stay,
For in my heart, I've found my way.

Marked

Marked by the meaning of life,
Carved in the depths, beyond all strife.
A mark that echoes through the years,
Whispered in silence, felt in fears.

Marked by the meaning of truth,
Rooted deeply in eternal youth.
A light that never fades away,
Guiding me through night and day.

Marked by the meaning of power,
Rising up like a blooming flower.
A force within, untamed and bright,
Shining strong through darkest night.

Marked by the meaning of symbolism,
A canvas painted with life's prism.
Each stroke, each hue, each careful line,
Reflects the sacred, divine design.

Marked by those who scorn and sour,
Yet, in their shadows, I find my power.
Their words may sting, but cannot break,
For I am forged in the fires I make.

I am marked by the heavens high,
A star that glows in the boundless sky.
My soul speaks in whispers, calm and true,
Imparting wisdom, as it grew.

Marked by the clues, the hues I see,
In every dawn, in every breeze.
A calmness held in every view,
A quiet strength that carries through.

For I am marked for the greater good,
A path I walk, misunderstood.
Marked as the creator of my fate,
Building my life with love, not hate.

I know nothing new, and not a foe,
Just a spirit that continues to grow.
For I am marked, forever to be,
A soul aligned with what's meant to be.

Minding My Business

Go away, for I am minding my own business,
A quiet space where peace meets stillness.
Don't distract me, don't pull me aside,
For in my solitude, my thoughts reside.

My work life swirls, a bustling tide,
But in the end, my heart finds pride,
In the simple act of being free—
Minding my own, just letting it be.

The mindfulness I hold is just for me,
A moment carved in quiet to see,
To feel the world with open grace,
To move at my own sacred pace.

For myself, I choose to hear,
The whispers soft, the thoughts sincere.
For myself, I listen close,
To the wisdom that I cherish most.

For myself, I touch the earth,
In every step, I find my worth.
For myself, I embrace the day,
With love, I gently pave my way.

For myself, I acknowledge truth,
The power found in quiet youth.
For myself, I stand my ground,
In my own space, where peace is found.

Not to be taken, nor to be led,
I walk my path, where thoughts are fed.
Let it be, let the world be still,
As I mind my business, free from ill.

So let me tend to my mystery,
A business built with quiet history.
Minding my own, with open eyes,
A soul unbound, beneath clear skies.

Playing Games

I am over with you playing games,
The endless cycle, always the same.
What once was fun now feels so tame,
A hollow dance, a fleeting flame.

Something I can't control, can't tame,
A streak of luck that fuels the aim,
A sudden twist, a roll of fate,
That sends you spinning, sealed by fate.

Meticulous, sharp, with fiery passion,
Executing moves, a perfect fashion.
Yet, in this game, there's something wrong,
A fleeting victory, but not for long.

For playing games can push you far,
To lands unknown, to touch a star.
But fame is fleeting, it fades away,
A bitter taste that won't decay.

I see the game and feel disdain,
The endless cycle, all in vain.
Transformed into a hermit's life,
Days wasted, caught in strife.

I'm over it, no more games,
No more chasing fleeting flames.
It's time to choose what's real, what's true,
To seek the life that's meant for you.

Boundaries set, they stand so tall,
A defense against the endless call.
The game no longer has a place,
It's time to step away from this race.

For the real game, the true pursuit,
Is not in play, but in the pursuit.
The boundaries are not a cage,
But a guide to step off the stage.

The game is in the living, you see,
In knowing what's worth to be free.
Playing games is no longer the same,
It's time to rise beyond the game.

When Toxic

When you are toxic, you are beside me,
A shadow that lingers, too close to be free.
You wear your poison like it's a crown,
And in your presence, I begin to drown.

When you are toxic, you cannot reside in me,
For the air I breathe becomes thick with debris.
I can't hold you close without losing my way,
Your venom seeps in, causing dismay.

When it gets toxic, it's a matter of time,
A decision to make, a choice to define.
To take out the trash, to clear the debris,
To set myself free from what used to be me.

The space we shared, now mashed and torn,
A place once warm, now tattered, worn.
I feel the weight, I feel the pain,
The echoes of the past that still remain.

It's more than a memory, more than a scar,
It's the moment we grew apart, so far.
Not just acknowledging, but understanding the split,
The shift that broke us, bit by bit.

I know it was harsh, the severing of ties,
But sometimes love means saying goodbye.
When toxic, you become the last,
A shadow fading, a memory cast.

And now I stand, without the weight,
No longer burdened by toxic fate.
For in releasing you, I find my peace,
And in this letting go, I find my release.

Defending Kingdom

It is my right in defending kingdom,
A duty bound by fate, not random.
I stand with strength, unbowed, unbroken,
A force unyielding, yet softly spoken.

It is my power to defend this land,
With steadfast heart and steady hand.
Through trials deep, through battles long,
I rise to right where I belong.

It is my fate in defending kingdom,
A journey carved with every rhythm.
Through valleys dark, through heights unknown,
I defend the crown, I claim my throne.

It is my testimony, a sacred vow,
To guard this realm, to honor now.
The echoes of truth in every word,
A promise kept, a line never blurred.

It is my heart space in defending kingdom,
A love that soars, a fire seldom dimmed.
Through every storm, through every plight,
I hold this land, and fight the fight.

For defending kingdom is more than might,
It is a reflection of love so bright.
I reflect peace in every stride,
I reflect stillness with hearts open wide.

I reflect truth in every breath,
A light to guide, a shield from death.
I reflect passion, burning clear,
A flame that conquers doubt and fear.

I reflect strength to do the task,
A force that asks for nothing but to bask
In the glory of what is just,
To shield the kingdom, to gain its trust.

My mission is clear, my purpose true,
To defend this kingdom through and through.
With every action, with every prayer,
I stand as one who will always care.

For in defending, I find my way,
Through night and dawn, through every day.
It is my right, my power, my grace,
To defend this kingdom, to take my place.

Thoughts of Affection

Your thoughts are my affection,
A gentle wave, a soft reflection.
In every thought, I find the grace,
A quiet love that fills the space.

Your thoughts reflect my affection,
A mirror held in sweet connection.
Each glance, each glance, each silent stare,
Becomes a whisper in the air.

Your thoughts deflect affection,
Yet still, they beckon my direction.
A dance of mind, a fleeting trace,
Love hidden in the quiet space.

Your thoughts send a projection to affection,
A beam of light, a warm direction.
Through every curve, through every bend,
The thought of love will never end.

Your thoughts, through strength and pride,
Where hearts and minds can both reside.
A fortress built with careful care,
In thoughts of affection, pure and rare.

I have power over thoughts of affection,
A gentle reign, a soft reflection.
Through every wave, through every tide,
I steer the ship with love as guide.

That leads to a mind of full perfection,
Where love is birthed in each connection.
A perfect world, so bright, so clear,
A realm where affection draws us near.

The beauty of thoughts of affection,
A light that warms the soul's complexion.
It calms the night full of dark connections,
Turning shadows into soft reflections.

For in these thoughts, a love is born,
A place where hearts are never torn.
In every thought, affection's light,\

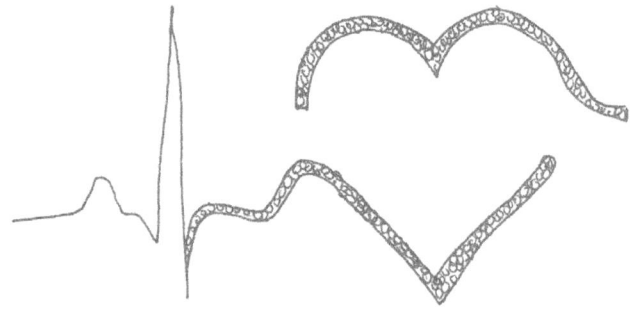

To Be the Creative

I am creative,
A spark that never fades,
A rhythm in my soul that quietly invades.
I wonder in the creative,
Lost in the flow of boundless dreams,
Where every thought, every vision, gleams.

I keep creative,
A flame that burns so bright,
In every corner, in the silent night.
I give what is creative,
A gift of light, a piece of my soul,
A song, a stroke, a vision whole.

I summon the creative,
With every breath, with every move,
A magic that stirs, a power to prove.
I know the creative,
It flows through me, it is my core,
A truth I seek, a light I adore.

I feel the creative,
In the whispers of the wind,
In the pulse of the earth, in the depths within.
I inspire the creative,
In others' hearts, it takes flight,
A dance, a dream, a spark so bright.

I cherish the creative,
A treasure found in every day,
In moments soft, in words we say.
The creative is divine,
A gift bestowed, a flame that burns,
A force of life, from which we learn.

The creative is a gift,
A blessing from the skies,
A reason to reach, a truth that never dies.
The creative has a purpose,
To heal, to guide, to show the way,
To lift us up, to help us sway.

The creative can uplift,
With hands that build, with words that soar,
A hope that heals, a heart restored.
The creative connects to the higher source,
A river that flows with wisdom deep,
A sacred bond, a promise we keep.

The creative has insight,
A vision born from deep inside,
It shows the path, where dreams reside.
The creative has plans,
A blueprint drawn in the stars,
A journey that takes us near and far.

The creative also experiences and overcomes storms,
In moments dark, it finds its form,
Through trials faced, through battles won,
It rises higher with the sun.

This is how I am creative,
A soul that soars, a heart that feels,
A spirit free, a world that heals.
To be creative,
Is to live with passion, to forever strive,
A light that shines, a way to thrive.

Paid to Exist

I am to exist,
A being of purpose, a soul unmissed.
I am paid to exist,
Not with coins, but with the grace that persists.
I make my own abundance,
Crafted from thoughts, with no hindrance.
Through the mentality of a hundred,
I rise, I soar, my spirit unencumbered.

So far I shall soar,
Beyond the limits, to heights I adore.
The evidence is clear, I am not spiritually poor,
For in my heart, abundance pours.
I am paid to exist because I am adored,
By heavens' grace, the source opens the doors.

The gateway to creative freedom is my reward,
A treasure found in the stillness, unexplored.
I am abundant by the hoards,
Voice echoing down the corridors,
A melody of life, a song I sing,
Making my life bliss, an eternal spring.

At ease, so as I appease,
I am paid to exist,
A life of peace, an endless mist.
I am heavenly teased,
By the whispers of the divine,
Each moment a gift, every breath a sign.

It is with such keys, to open these doors,
To be freed, to be more,
A path laid before me, so pure,
I step forward, with heart secure.
For I am paid to exist,
A divine life, an eternal bliss.

Lovesick Puppy

You have become my lovesick puppy,
With eyes that gleam so brightly, lovely.
I adored the way you looked at me,
Like I was the one you longed to see.
Your gaze, so deep, so pure, so true,
Like a lovesick puppy, I was drawn to you.

You praised me, raised me on a pedestal high,
Like a lovesick puppy, you'd never ask why.
You saw me as your dream, your queen,
Your love for me, so tender, unseen.
With every word, with every glance,
You made me feel like I was your only chance.

You gazed into my eyes, adoringly,
With all your heart's desire, so passionately.
Abhorring any doubts, any fears,
You loved me through the passing years.
Like a lovesick puppy, so innocent, so sweet,
Your love for me was endless, complete.

You kissed me, mesmerizing the night,
Like a lovesick puppy, everything felt right.
Every touch, every caress, every embrace,
Felt like a gentle, tender grace.
Like a lovesick puppy, you held me near,
Whispering promises, sweet and clear.

You were always by my side,
Like a lovesick puppy, your heart open wide.
No distance, no time could tear us apart,
For you held me close within your heart.
Our love was enchanted, moving with grace,
Like a lovesick puppy, I found my place.

A love so full, so wild, so free,
Like a lovesick puppy, forever we'll be.
In your gaze, I see the world anew,
For I, too, am lovesick, just for you

Keep It

Just keep it,
Keep it to yourself,
Let it dwell in the corners of your soul,
For some things are better left untold.
No one has to know,
No need for their gaze to follow,
Let your secrets quietly grow,
Untouched by others' hands, hollow.

No one has to intervene,
To meddle in the spaces serene,
In my growth, in my stride,
Let me rise with nothing to hide.
No one has to understand,
The wisdom that I've built with my hand,
For my gifts are mine to shape,
Not theirs to take.

No one has to regret,
For their actions have no debt,
To intervene on my territory,
Is to alter my story.
No one has to believe,
What they can't see, can't conceive,
For my thoughts are my own to hold,
Not for their judgments to unfold.

No one has to see,
The essence of what makes me free,
For talents bloom in quiet space,
Not for the world to chase.
No one has to stop,
To limit the heights that I can hop,
For my worth is not theirs to define,
It's set in stone, it's purely mine.

No one has to care,
To cross the lines that I declare,
My boundaries are strong and true,
For they are drawn by me, not you.
No one has to take the hard road,
In the journey where my heart glowed,
To honor oneself is to stand alone,
To keep it all, and make it known.

So keep it,
Let it rest within your soul,
For peace is found when you take control,
Of what is yours to keep and cherish,
A self-bound journey that will never perish.

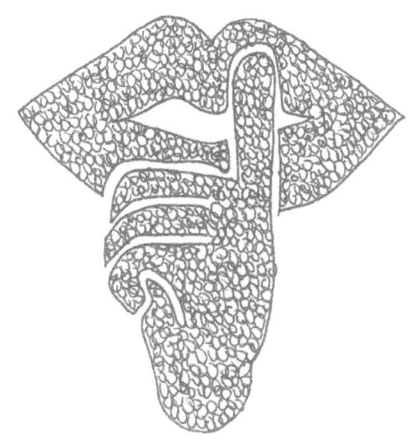

More Prosperous

I am more prosperous than you think,
In the blink of an eye, I start to sink—
Into the depths of my own light,
Where possibilities soar and take flight.
This is no lie, there is a link,
A secret connection that makes me think.
I may as well send you a wink,
A sign of the future, a glimpse, a blink.

I am more prosperous to the naked eye,
What cannot be seen is not a stye.
In the depths of my soul, I see the sky,
A canvas where my dreams can fly.
I have a promise written in my nature,
Etched in the stars, the sun, the sky's true stature.
A legacy born of eternal desire,
To reach higher and higher, never to tire.

I am more prosperous and always wise,
In every challenge, I rise.
There's no stopping what's bound to be,
The flow of abundance surrounding me.
I have nothing of despise,
For the heart that loves is rich in size.
To love and learn, a prosperous quest,
A journey where the soul finds its rest.

The heart will earn and yearn,
For the great prosperous highs to return.
In the giving and taking, in every leap,
I find what I sow is what I reap.
For I am more prosperous than I've ever known,
A beacon of light, an eternal stone.

Even More

I think even more than you can believe,
Deeper than words or a quiet reprieve.
I think of you more than a simple glance,
Your eyes that scan every sleeve in a trance.
I think even more than the tan of your skin,
I think of you beyond what's seen from within.
A love so docile, an innocent hymn,
A soft melody that plays on a whim.

I am meant for the bewilderment, the wonder,
A journey through life, where hearts do not blunder.
A faint tint in the distance, a shadowed glow,
Yet in this quiet love, our hearts freely flow.
This love that soars, even more high,
Beyond the sun, the stars, and the sky.
Between my heart, even more when we grow apart,
The distance only deepens this love in my heart.

There is even more than I have left in my art,
A canvas of emotions, a masterpiece to start.
Even more to the haste, the rush of desire,
A love-led war that will never tire.
Even more than the battles we choose to fight,
The journey continues into the endless night.
And at the end, an encore, a new start,
For there is even more in the depths of my heart.

Star of the Show

I know you think I am the star of the show,
The one who shines, the one you know.
I know you acknowledge my greatness, so true,
A debt of respect, a tribute from you.
I know you see my talents unfold,
Like a story told in whispers, bold.

I know you feel my fame in the air,
Like a fragrance of success, floating there.
I know you smell a winner in disguise,
Not to jeopardize my name, nor tell lies.
I know you feel the bitterness, a sting,
From the times I denied what you wished to bring.

But not to fret, no need to sigh,
For in my silence, my spirit can fly.
I know, I know, I am the star of the show,
A quiet achiever, with grace to bestow.
I know, I know, my rewards come from deep within,
My creativity, my heart, where dreams begin.

I know, I know, I've been put in a place,
To listen, to grow, to accept my grace.
I am of faith, responsibility, love, and praise,
Facing the opposition in all their gaze.
For I know, I am the star of the show,
A juxtaposition, with strength to grow.

In shadows or light, in whispers or cries,
I rise, I rise, a star in the skies

www.ingramcontent.com/pod-product-compliance
Lightning Source LLC
Chambersburg PA
CBHW041309110526
44590CB00028B/4308